Usborne

First Sticker Book

Nature

Illustrated by Federica Iossa

Designed by Francesca Allen

Words by Felicity Brooks

Contents

Expert advice from Dr. John Rostron
and Dr. Margaret Rostron

You will find all the stickers
at the back of the book.

Deep in the woods

When no one's around, lots of animals come out to eat and play in this European forest. Add them to this scene.

On the African plains

Fill these plains with giraffes, rhinos, lions and elephants.
Which other animals come to the watering hole to drink?

A coral reef

A coral reef is the undersea home of all kinds of amazing fish. Add lots more to this picture. Find a place for an octopus and a turtle, too.

By the forest

You'll find bears, wolves and owls in a North American pine forest. How many animals can you add to this scene?

The Arctic

It's always freezing cold in the Arctic, but plenty of animals live here.
Add some whales, a polar bear and a walrus to this icy scene.

At the seashore

Take a look under the water in this seaside rock pool. Can you stick on some more sea anemones and starfish? Add some seashore birds to this picture, too.

In the Jungle

Monkeys, macaws, sloths and jaguars all make their home in the Amazon Jungle. Add them all to the picture.

A garden pond

Fill the pond with frogs, toads and pond snails.
Add dragonflies and butterflies to the picture, too.

Deep in the woods (pages 2-3)

Bank vole

Jay

Rabbit

Blackbird

Tawny owl

Jay

Great spotted woodpecker

Ferns

Speckled wood butterfly

Roe deer

Badger

Roe deer

Hedgehog

Mouse

Shrew

Roe deer

Squirrel

Fox

Great spotted woodpecker

Fox and fox cub

Rabbit

Weasel

On the African plains
(pages 4-5)

Vulture

Cheetah

Giraffe

Lion cub

Impala

Weaverbird

Cattle egret

Zebra

Kudu

Hippopotamus

Ostrich

Aardvark

Warthog

Elephant

Acacia tree

Termite mound

Leopard

Baby elephant

Lion

Rhinoceros

Striped mongoose

A coral reef (pages 6-7)

Common octopus

Emperor angelfish

Masked pufferfish

Blue spotted stingray

Red Sea clownfish

Sea goldies

Dugong

Hermit crab

Giant moray eel

Squirrelfish

Fire coral

Red Sea clownfish

Orange cup coral

Lionfish

Picasso triggerfish

Masked butterfly fish

Sea turtle

Coral grouper

By the forest
(pages 8-9)

Pine marten

Owl

Brown bear

Lynx

American porcupine

Flying squirrel

White-tailed deer

Long-eared owl

Crossbill

Skunk

Red squirrel

Chipmunk

Moose

Beaver

Wolf

Musk ox

Polar bear

Ptarmigan

Lemmings

Humpback
whale

Caribou

Arctic fox

Polar bear
cubs

Stoat

Snowy owl

Killer whale

Arctic hare

Baby harp seal

Ptarmigan

Gyrfalcon

Walrus

Raven

Arctic wolf

At the seashore
(pages 12-13)

Oystercatcher

Puffin

Bladderwrack seaweed

Dogwhelk

Razorbill

Cormorant

Redshank

Beadlet anemone

Limpets

Beadlet anemone

Starfish

Snakelocks anemone

Acorn barnacles

Common periwinkles

Edible sea urchin

Starfish

Crab

Blennies

In the Jungle (pages 14-15)

Sun parakeet

Toco toucan

Marpesia marcella
butterfly

Emerald
tree boa

Common squirrel monkey

Woolly
monkey

Scarlet macaw

Three-toed sloth
and baby sloth

Spider
monkey

Blue morpho
butterfly

Golden lion tamarin

Armadillo

Jaguar

A garden pond (page 16)

Butterfly

Mole

Toad

Yellow iris

Frogs

Dragonflies

Small white butterfly

Pond snail

Pond skaters

Water lily

Lily pad

Use these extra stickers in any way you want.